CATCHING GREATNESS

A GUIDE TO THRIVING IN A WORLD PLAGUED BY GRAVITY

Copyright © Niels Duinker 2014

ISBN 978-90-821676-1-0

First edition, first impression 2014

Cover design by Ruud van Eijk
Printed and bound by CreateSpace

All rights reserved. No part of this publication may be reproduced, stored in a retrieval system, or transmitted, in any form or by any means, electronic, mechanical, photocopying, recording or otherwise, without the prior written permission of the copyright holder.

I would like to thank Annie Keeling and Barry Friedman for all the help and support in the creation of this book.

Table of Contents

Introduction   7

Ten Inspirational Events and What You Can Do (Starting NOW!)   9
- 1. A Big Aha! I Could Get Paid for What I Loved   9
- 2. Street Performing for the First Time   10
- 3. Surviving a Test, Building Character   12
- 4. Attending My First Juggling Convention   13
- 5. National Table Tennis Competition   15
- 6. Meeting Jason Garfield, a Juggling Celebrity   16
- 7. Circus Belly Wien   18
- 8. Audition for Cirque du Soleil   20
- 9. Lunch with the Prince and Princess of the Netherlands   22
- 10. Theme Park "Huis Ten Bosch" Japan   24

Early Impactful Experiences   29
- Where I Grew Up   31
- My Parents   33
- Childhood   35
- University   37
- Travel   39

Successful Influences — 43
- The "Best" – Anthony Gatto and Jason Garfield — 43
- Christopher Rodogell – Juggler and Choreographer — 44
- Steve Jobs on Strategy — 46
- Valentino Bihorac – Future Inspiration — 46
- Many Mentors in Many Places — 47
- Kaskade Magazine — 53

Life Strategies or How to Take Control of Your Life — 55
- Find a Passion or Purpose — 55
- Peer Pressure — 57
- Social Media — 58
- Unhealthy Distractions — 59
- Voices of Negativity — 60
- Boredom – Get Off the Couch — 61
- Overcoming Fear — 62
- Change and How to Deal With It — 63
- Organizational Skills — 64
- Using Resources Well — 65
- Seeking Information — 66
- Applying What You Learn — 66
- Speaking to People You Don't Know — 68
- No Prima Donnas — 69

Character Traits That Lead to Success — 72
- Weighing the Opinion of Others — 72
- Persistence — 72
- Physical Character — 74
- Mental Character — 76
- Emotional Character — 76
- On Success — 77
- Taking Action — 78

BONUS – Learn to Juggle — 80
Suggested Resources — 83
Niels Duinker's Resume — 87
Acknowledgements — 107

Introduction

"I'm not telling you it's going to be easy.
I'm telling you it's going to be worth it." —*Anonymous*

My name is Niels Duinker. I was born in Rotterdam in the Netherlands in 1985. You can see by the cover of the book that I am a performer and juggler. I have performed all over Europe, in Asia, and made special guest appearances in the United States. I travel extensively all over the world performing high-profile engagements at theatres, casinos, cruise ships, theme parks, and corporate events.

My life often seems like a charmed existence and many have told me that I am "lucky." Maybe that is true. A series of inspirations came my way that affected me deeply. But it has also taken a lot of hard work to get where I am.

When I got the idea to write this book, I thought of all the young people I know. Some are very motivated to follow a passion or a specific path and just need some pointed guidance to help them stay the course. Others need a gentle nudge to go in a particular direction. And still others need a big push from an inspirational model that helps them take even one small step.

In the first section, *10 Inspirational Events and What You Can Do (Starting NOW)*, I have listed actions that you can take right away toward your own success. I suggest you grab a notebook because you will want to make lists and take notes about your personal experience and toward your future growth. I have included my background and influences to show you what has worked for me. I hope to inspire you to take your own positive steps. You'll also want to keep your notebook handy for the section titled, *Life Strategies or How to Take Control of Your Life*, in which you'll have another opportunity to get specific about actions in your life.

There is no magic formula or lucky success leprechaun, but there is making the most of all that comes across your path.

> **"One secret of success in life is for a man to be ready for his opportunity when it comes."** —*Benjamin Disraeli*

On my way to one of my very first gigs

CHAPTER 1

10 Inspirational Events and What You Can Do (Starting NOW!)

1. A Big Aha! I Could Get Paid for What I Loved

When I was 13 years old, I was invited to perform two shows—and get paid for them! For the first one, some neighbors a few blocks down from where I lived threw a BBQ with the entire street. One family organized the BBQ and everybody chipped in and helped. The organizer saw me juggling in the local playground and invited me over.

I got my second gig through someone who saw me at the BBQ. They invited me to perform at the "Award Ceremony" of the coloring contest on the children's ward of the local hospital. I asked to be paid 7 gulden (about 7 USD) for the show and got 10. On top of the pay, I got another gig so I thought I was killing it.

The payment wasn't "awesome" but still, I was proud of getting paid. It equaled what my friends made for working 3 hours in the super market and the gigs turned out to be a good experience. It would cost me about 2 hours of work to get myself over there, do the show, and to get back. Also, I was proud that I could select the show material myself instead of being told what to do by a manager at the supermarket.

What I learned
This was an eye-opening experience. I could get paid for something I enjoyed and not have to work for someone else, either. This was important in helping to shape my way of looking at work and business.

Taking It Home
Look for a passion in life. What you love doing may be something that someone else cannot do or actually hates to do. Think with an entrepreneurial spirit instead of doing only what you are told.

2. Street Performing for the First Time

My first time street performing, also known as *busking*, was a scary experience. I was 14 years old. The professional street performers that I saw every year at the Rotterdam Street Performing Festival were all doing it. I decided that I wanted to do it, too. I looked up to them and I felt I could only get the same experience and respect if I took the same steps.

When I started out I didn't know any other performers. People in my neighborhood and area were joking around that I should go out on the street and put a hat in front of me. As I think back, those people were likely not as serious about their statements as I took them. I thought that I *should* do it and if I didn't, I would lose out on something cool.

It was time to take action. I went to the local shopping area and thought, "Let's dive straight in." But when I stopped walking and arrived at my *pitch*, I got nervous and picked my bag up again. (The area where a street performance occurs is called a *pitch*.)

After a few years I got pretty good at street performing...

I had told people that I would do it. If I went home then without having done it, I would feel like a liar and a fake. I didn't like that option. So I walked around the shopping mall for about 10 minutes and decided to do it again. It was really scary. I decided to perform until one person gave me some money and then immediately go home thereafter. That way I really could say I did it (not very successfully), but at least I would have done it. And I would have made "some money." So I could say "yes" when people asked me if I had done it and made money.

What I learned
This profoundly changed me. Here's some take-aways from the experience:
- It was a real "smack in the face" toward taking action. All my words didn't count if I didn't take action. When I meet young aspiring performers, I tell them to take action. It is better to start and not get the full success that you are hoping for on your first attempt. Just start and stay real.
- Street performing started my career and was an opportunity to learn more. Those early street shows gave me invaluable lessons that are not being taught at any professional circus school.
- Real audience feedback was gold. I got to see what the audience liked or not. It also gave me peeks into human nature. For example, immigrants that some people talk badly about put the most money in my hat. "Successful people" with expensive shoes or clothes gave me only a few cents and were rude half of the time. These realizations made it easier to see that the "success" of performing on TV, etc. doesn't mean too much in the end. The people that are impressed by those shows the most are the people that were the rudest to me when I started out street performing.
- Juggling changed from being purely a hobby to my part-time job. I thought it was quite cool. Most friends had a hobby that only cost them (or their parents) money. My hobby paid for itself. Making money from my hobby allowed me to pursue my biggest passion: buying more and better juggling props.

Taking It Home
What risk are you afraid to take? What risk is keeping you from getting to a place of success? You have to fail many times before you can ever have success. What risk can you take that will count as one of your failures which will eventually lead you to success? Start taking action now.

Juggling fire at age 14

3. Surviving a Test, Building Character

Jugglers need a lot of props—balls, clubs, rings, unicycles, etc. Most of the props I purchased, I earned myself. I had to pay for my very first set of good juggling balls with my weekly allowance. I think my father wanted to test my desire to pursue juggling.

A few months later, I got my first set of juggling clubs as a gift from my parents. I was really saving up for those. The juggling clubs were supposed to be a present for my birthday (August 9th), but I got them a few weeks early (start of the summer holidays). My parents were worried that I had already saved up enough and would go out and buy a set myself. That reminds me of a story about one of the more advanced juggling props: torches.

The point of torches is that they are lit, allowing a performer to juggle fire. I wanted to juggle torches but my mother didn't like that idea. She said that I should learn to juggle better first and I was only allowed to buy those torches if I could juggle 5 clubs. She thought that I would never be able to do that since only one professional juggler in Rotterdam could juggle 5 clubs back then.

This was upsetting to me. I mentioned that her rationale didn't make sense at all. My friends from the youth circus could only juggle 3 clubs and their parents allowed them to juggle with fire. All without injury, I explained. My mother didn't agree. So I set to practicing harder. After a year or so I could juggle 5 clubs. My mother still didn't like for me to juggle fire but I had done my part of the deal so I could buy the torches.

What I learned
In the above story, I got my mother's buy-in. She basically was saying, if you can play bigger, I can support you more. I used her challenge as an inspiration to work harder toward my goal.

Taking It Home
Invite people in your life to see you as someone who can play bigger. Look for challenges where you may least expect them.

4. Attending My First Juggling Convention

When I was 14 years old, I heard about a one-day juggling convention that was being held close to where I lived. The location was 1.5 hours away by public transportation. I had never travelled all by myself on a train before. I had only used the subway system of Rotterdam alone. This was going to be a new experience.

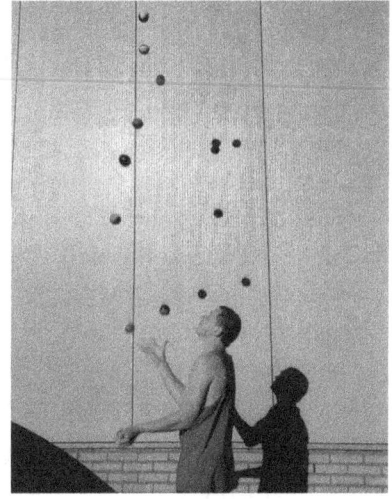

Above: Me juggling 9 balls at the Dutch Juggling Convention in 2001
Left: Anthony Gatto at the Circus Festival of Monte-Carlo in 2000

14 10 Inspirational Events And What You Can Do (Starting NOW!)

With my friend Jasper Riedeman during the games at the Dutch Juggling Convention 2000

I thought that at a "real" juggling festival, all the jugglers must be very good. I could only juggle with 4 balls by that time and I thought I would really be nothing if I couldn't juggle 5 balls. As I had seen on the television show, *The Circus Festival of Monte-Carlo*, the real jugglers all juggled extremely well.

I had only one month to prepare. So I set the goal for myself to learn to juggle 5 balls in that month. When it came close to the date of the juggling convention I realized that a solid pattern wouldn't be possible for me within the remaining time frame. But 20 catches would be possible and it still would leave the impression of being close to juggling 5 balls. I would be able to show the really good jugglers that I would have the potential of learning this skill.

When I made it to the juggling festival, I noticed that only a handful of jugglers could juggle 5 balls over there. By assuming that the bar would be much higher than it was in real life I pushed myself harder. I actually learned to juggle 5 balls much faster than others because of this approach.

What I learned
If you shoot for the sun but you don't make it to the sun and land on the moon, you still have made it to the moon. And if you don't shoot at all, you end up staying home.

Taking It Home
Set a goal with the intention of not necessarily achieving it, but working toward it with an amount of attention that is beyond what you would do without the goal. This will push you farther each time.

5. National Table Tennis Competition

Between the ages of 8 and 12 years old, I was really enthusiastic about playing table tennis. Twice a week I went to the table tennis club to practice. I was thinking about table tennis all the time. In my room I had created a mini-table from two plates of wood that I had found in our attic and another piece of wood served as the net.

Whenever my friend came over, we practiced on this small table that I placed on the floor in my bedroom. When he wasn't there, sometimes I used the wall as my sparring partner. Eventually, I joined a team at the table tennis club to start playing competitions.

One time our coach took us to a national table tennis tournament. I thought that everybody would be really good just "because they were from far away." I had been placed in a category of kids with more experience so I didn't win my matches, but I still provided tough competition for

Practicing table tennis

my opponents. My coach was proud. At the end of the day, I realized that distance didn't automatically equal good. Conversely, I was far away to the opponents. I realized that it was the actual amount of practice somebody put in—not their appearance, location, etc. that mattered or made a difference.

What I learned
The lesson for me was not to let my preconceptions stop me, but to inspire me toward improvement and mastery. I also had the opportunity to realize I could be a confident participant and didn't need to be intimidated by my own expectations.

Taking It Home
Look at the places in your life where you hold judgments or stereotypes, which may not serve you to be your best. The easiest thing in the world is to look at someone's ability or achievement and use that to discourage you. My challenge is for this to inspire you instead. You could go so far as to even contact that person and let them know you will use them as inspiration instead of discouragement. Take this action step: List a place right now where you are stopping yourself because you don't think that you are good enough.

6. Meeting Jason Garfield, a Juggling Celebrity

In 2001, the European Juggling Convention (EJC) had been organized in Rotterdam. Because of some of the tourist attractions of nearby Amsterdam, a lot of jugglers from Spain, Italy and all over all came to the convention, making it the biggest juggling festival that had ever been held until then. The organization hadn't taken into account the appeal of the tourist attractions in Amsterdam. There was much better attendance than expected. The European Juggling Association always allowed the host juggling club to keep a part of the profit of all related activities. This created a nice amount of extra money for our club.

Two of my early influences were jugglers Anthony Gatto and Jason Garfield. I had been watching their juggling videotapes on a daily basis for over two years. On Jason Garfield's website I read about his "Practice 'Till You Puke Workshop." I didn't know what this expression (puke)

10 Inspirational Events And What You Can Do (Starting NOW!)   17

Talking with Jason Garfield after his show in Rotterdam in 2001

meant but just to get lessons from a juggling master sounded like the best thing in the world.

With the left-over/profit money from the EJC and the lack of energy of the organization to use it for another festival, I persuaded them to book Jason Garfield to come over from LA and do a 4-day master workshop. I was 17 years old by then and had just finished high school. Now that I think back on it and compare it with other 17-year-olds I knew, I am quite impressed that it worked out and my thought became a reality. At the time, it sounded really logical and there was no reason why it shouldn't work.

I spent four days showing Jason Garfield around and learned a lot. It was also the first time I met a "celebrity" and in the end, I came to the conclusion that celebrities are just like regular people. They can have weird habits, get nervous sometimes, and sometimes they disappoint you. It was a great experience overall and without the effort Jason Garfield has put into juggling, I wouldn't be where I am today.

What I learned
- One big take-away from this experience was that celebrities are people too and not demigods. This has helped me later on as I have attained more success and have had the privilege of meeting many celebrities. When

I do a TV show where I share the bill with one of them, I no longer get nervous. Also, I realize that when I am on-stage, some people will see me as a celebrity. I have the responsibility of being remembered for my personality and respectful behavior, above all.

- There is also the possibility that one of your heroes isn't who you thought they were. What happened for me is that a barrier broke away in my brain and I started thinking about how I could still honor the greatness in my hero. I came to the conclusion that what I didn't like in him/her could inspire me to strive for the greater things and add to my own life where I believed the hero had failed.

Taking It Home
Write down some ways that you have been inspired by others and the qualities that you admire. Then, write down ways that you could inspire others in your field and peripherally as well, considering the ripples out to people who may also be inspired by you.

7. Circus Belly Wien

During the Christmas season of 2011, I got offered to perform with Circus Belly Wien at The Rijnhal in the city of Arnhem in the Netherlands. I was offered this contract through my friend, Christopher Rodogell who had started a talent agency. Christopher is from the circus world and had heard that Circus Belly Wien was looking for a juggler for their Christmas show. He helped me put together a new act and thought this would be a good opportunity to polish it.

My friend knew that the circus director of Circus Belly Wien was a bit shady. When I arrived, there were no accommodations for me, the circus wanted to charge me for my food and drinks, and I didn't get a dressing room. I already had agreed on getting paid at the end of each show since I had tried to work at the circus once before and had been taken advantage of then as well. The circus director was a huge man and really strong (from setting up tents). It took me some courage to tell the circus director that I was going to leave if he did not live up to his commitments. He told me that the rumors were true—that he didn't always pay during the regular season, but this was Christmas after all... Yeah, sure!!

I walked out of the circus and when I was waiting for the taxi, I checked my email on my cell phone. There was an email from Cirque du Soleil. The timing was so unreal. I had been hoping to get an email from Cirque du Soleil for a while. It was like the universe wanted to tell me something.

What I learned
- If it doesn't feel good, don't do it.
- Be aware of laziness. It's not good for business.
- Be careful when doing business with friends.
- It is also important to listen to your inner voice. Personally, I feel sensations in my chest and stomach that affirm what my brain is thinking. Important decisions like picking the right high school, University, direction of my career, and certain investments have not been based on numbers and statistics. I "feel" that I should choose them.
- There are two sides of the brain: the brain that operates on fear (fight or flight) and the one that operates on intuition and listening to your gut. The latter often goes against what others might be advising you to do.
- The Hawaiian's have a word that helps describe this: Na'au.

"The na'au are the guts or intestines; the word is also used to mean instinct, a person's gut-level feelings and intuition."
—from: http://www.managingwithaloha.com/glossary/

It is here that the seat of wisdom and intelligence, emotion, and physical strength is believed to reside. The expression "gut feeling" reflects the understanding that this is the core of our being, the seat of emotion.

After I make a gut-level decision, I realize that there is no way I could change it and I have to go for it. I also realize that there is only one time that I am 18 years old. There is only one time that I am 25 years old, etc. So I better make the best out of that situation during that time in my life.

I try to remember all of this when I am in difficult situations or making decisions.

Taking It Home
Practice listening to your intuition in small circumstances. Take small steps in trusting it. Soon that will lead to huge steps that you would have never taken if you had depended on the fight/flight brain.

8. Audition for Cirque du Soleil

February 2012, I went to Paris to audition for Cirque du Soleil. The audition was being held at the Circus School Fratellini, a famous circus school. It was amazing to receive this invitation just 10 minutes after my decision to walk out of Circus Belly Wien. The timing of that email was perfect for me.

I was not sure if I actually wanted to perform with a 7-minute act in one of the Cirque du Soleil shows but I was proud to be invited anyway. My main goal was to get a letter of recommendation from them stating my skills were "Cirque du Soleil" quality. I thought that getting a letter like that from them would open up more opportunities in my career than working for them.

Tons of artists apply for Cirque du Soleil and I had the privilege of being selected to audition. I arrived at the audition with a big bag of props, most of which I use in my standard 45-minute cruise ship set. In the letter of invitation, it stated that each artist had to prepare their "best material". All the material that I do in my show is something I want to be so proud of that I can perform on stage anywhere (even prestigious gigs).

A few weeks before the audition, I had seen an HBO series called *Bullshit* from Penn & Teller. They explained that "the best" didn't exist. After the Circus Belly Wien disaster, I hoped that the number one circus in the world would do everything right. If something doesn't exist how can you ask for it? I would have found it more fair if the letter would have stated, "Prepare an act that you think will get you hired."

That got me thinking about trying something different. At the audition, I put all the props in front of me. I did my 5-ball routine and thereafter I opened my mouth. I was the only act that spoke and did comedy during the audition piece.

"I read in the letter that you are looking for my best material," I said. "But what I think you're looking for is the best match of material with what you have an opening for, because something that will fit in one of your shows is only something you will book. On the floor you see all the props that I can perform with. You know what you're looking for so please tell me what you would like me to show you next."

That confused the audition panel. After exchanging bewildered looks,

In Paris the day after the audition for Cirque du Soleil

they decided on the hats. I thought it would be funny if I said, "Sorry, that is the only prop I can't do. I just decided to throw that in to impress you even more." So I did. That got an uncomfortable laugh from the other artists watching, who didn't know if laughing would actually be appropriate. I did my hat routine and if it had been a regular show I would say it went well regarding the audience.

Right before the lunch break, the audition panel announced some names of artists they would like to see more of and names of those they had seen enough and they could go home. I could go home. A girl who practiced aerial could go home as well and she was crying with disappointment.

Before leaving the building, each artist received individual feedback from the senior talent scout. I was told that they would have loved to see me juggling the clubs because that is something they were looking for. I asked why they simply hadn't asked for that and told them I could still show them club juggling. But no, my five minutes were over and I would have to submit a video now.

I asked the talent scout how much I could expect to earn at Cirque du Soleil to see if I would make the effort and submit the video and/or let the talent scout present my material to Cirque Eloize as well. After this audition, the talent scout emailed me at least five times, asking if I knew certain types of acts to recommend. I went to the audition to possibly end up working for the number one circus in the world myself and ended up being a source that they contacted afterwards to help them to find certain acts that their casting department couldn't find (female jugglers etc.).

What I learned
- Sometimes you go for something with the focus on one thing and you end up with the gold that results from an angle you didn't expect at all. Being in touch with the Cirque du Soleil organization is more valuable to me than working in their shows. I have my own show already and I have the artistic freedom to change my own act whenever I want. I would have had to follow the artistic vision of the director in Cirque du Soleil.
- Currently, I perform on-board Disney Cruise Lines. Cirque du Soleil and Disney are some of the biggest brands in entertainment worldwide. I have opened the door (just a little) to possibly become part of the organizational team of Cirque du Soleil. If that doesn't turn out to happen, at least I have the confidence that comes from knowing, after having been contacted so many times for additional information, that I can be of value to them. I went to audition to be a juggler and ended up an on-call consultant.

Taking It Home
Suppose there is something you want and you think you have an idea what it will look like when it comes. It's great for you put it out there, tell other people, and look for it. But be open for it to come in a package that is unlike anything that you expected. You may get an opportunity that's even bigger than you first imagined.

9. Lunch with the Prince and Princess of the Netherlands

In March, 2012, the International Magicians Society (IMS) awarded me, "Variety Act of the Year 2012." The president of the IMS came over from New York to Amsterdam to present the award to me. Two national TV shows came to film it. I was also invited to appear on a popular radio show.

The King and Queen of the Netherlands

After receiving this award, I received a lot of national TV coverage in the Netherlands and got invited to almost every talk show. The Prince and Princess of the Netherlands (now our King and Queen) host a luncheon at the palace where they invite about 30 guests who have recently received a major award in their profession. When I received the invitation I thought, "Who of my friends is playing a joke on me?" But there was a stamp on the letter and none of my friends would have put that much effort into it.

When I went to the palace, I met the Prince and Princess and had lunch with them. The prince gave a speech to welcome us all. He said that he was proud of every single member in the room and was honored for us to represent our country. It was also an honor having us represent the Netherlands internationally, and he hoped that everyone would keep doing the best in his profession. We should all continue to push ourselves and not be ashamed to be a role model.

When I started out, not many people believed that my goal of becoming a professional juggler would be possible. It was a great moment to hear the king say this personally. No higher recognition is possible. For years, all the skeptics I had met told me that I should have a back-up plan (like University) in case the juggling didn't work out. And then, here was the Prince saying that the country needed everybody's talents in the room.

In the past, I had sometimes felt ashamed that I pursued my passion, was working at it full-time, and was not using my formal school education. The government invests a lot of money into the Universities and I had taken time from the professors to get my Mechanical Engineering degree. After hearing this royal approval, I knew it was okay that I didn't professionally use my degree.

What I learned
The lesson is to do what you want to do with passion. Follow this regardless of the dissenters you may encounter. That way you can become the best, live in your genius, and be of service to more people with a higher standard and quality of work.

Taking It Home
Trust your gut and your inner wisdom. In a country of people that operate mostly by making decisions with their frontal lobe, I was with the prince and princess because I trusted my gut.

10. Theme Park Huis Ten Bosch Japan

In 2003, Jason Garfield gave me juggling lessons in Holland. In 2004, Jason got me over to the USA for the World Juggling Festival (WJF) convention that he had organized at the Riviera Hotel Casino in Las Vegas. It was my first invitation to the USA and in Las Vegas, no less!

The week after that competition in Las Vegas, another juggler named Scotty Cavanaugh had to leave for Japan to perform with his solo show at the largest theme park in the country: Huis Ten Bosch. Huis Ten Bosch is a Dutch village in Nagasaki and many entertainers have performed at that park.

I saw a documentary about that park on Dutch television when I was a little kid. I remember thinking, "Wow, that would be great to visit some day. It looks amazing."

In 2006, I visited Scotty in San Diego after the International Jugglers Association Festival that summer. When I stood with Scotty on the beach,

10 Inspirational Events And What You Can Do (Starting NOW!) 25

Painting of my shows at Huis Ten Bosch that artist Misaki Fukuda gave me as a present

26 10 Inspirational Events And What You Can Do (Starting NOW!)

Left: In San Diego with World Champion juggler Scotty Cavanaugh, 2006
Right: Juggling 7 clubs in theme park Huis Ten Bosch in Nagasaki

it was the first time that I had ever seen the Pacific Ocean. Until then I had only seen the North Sea. This was a REAL ocean. It is quite funny that all the maps of the world show the USA on the left side and end with Japan on the right. A lot of sea is cut out. So I had a feeling that Japan would be relatively close. I asked Scotty, "If you just keep swimming or sailing, would you end up in Japan?" He found that humorous.

I had always hoped to see Japan for myself. When I stood on that beach, I made myself a promise to go there. I felt it would be a big empty gap on my resume if I hadn't worked in Japan. Many great jugglers had worked in Japan: Dick Franco, Claudius Specht, Freddy Kenton, Dave Parker, Anthony Gatto and other excellent jugglers—so I wanted to go there as well. It was cool to see the palace where the Dutch queen lives in real life as well. Also the Dutch ship that discovered Nagasaki left from Rotterdam. That was 400 years ago. I live very close to Rotterdam. When I traveled to the park I thought it was awesome to do the same route as the first ship that went to Asia and started the Golden Age for the Dutch. And then, when I later got invited to lunch with the Royal family, I got to meet the King of the Netherlands who had grown up at the real Palace Huis Ten Bosch in Holland.

Hanging out on our day off with Mayuko

When I returned home from my trip to San Diego, I contacted the theme park, Huis Ten Bosch. I used the same strategy I used to book local street theatre festivals in Holland. I emailed the general email address of the park and asked for whoever was in charge of booking the acts. I then emailed the booker and asked why they always booked American acts if they had a Dutch theme park. I was a juggler from Holland and I would love to send them my promotional video. They agreed to that.

I went to film a special promo video in the city of Delft (where my University was). The architecture in that city was exactly like the park (an old Dutch village). So I sent that off and included a post card of Holland. I wrote on the post card, "I would like to present to you my promotional video. I hope you can imagine how it might look to have me juggling in your park."

My friend, James Bustar, was working at Huis Ten Bosch around that time. By coincidence, he was in the boss's office when the entertainment department watched my promo video. He said that they cracked up and loved it.

In the fall of 2007, I found myself in Japan. During that contract, I had the best period in my life. It probably helped, too, that this was the first time that a girl took my focus away. Her name was Mayuko. She worked at the theme park as an emcee of various game shows. She scheduled her breaks to be able to see many of my stage shows.

Japan can be really confusing when one first arrives due to the language, the signs, etc. It happened that she and I had the same day off. I said I wanted to go the city of Nagasaki (about 2 hours away by train) and she wanted to guide me. It was really interesting to spend time with a Japanese girl who was also very friendly, supportive, beautiful, and helpful.

Her English was okay, but not perfect, and that was quite cute. She was really confident but also could play "innocent girly" according to the Japanese culture. Sometimes she would give me a hard time for eating American junk food, telling me to eat more vegetables. We spent some good times together.

What I learned
The biggest lesson is to dream big and act on it... it just might work out. I made it easy for the people who could help by showing exactly what the scenario would look like. I didn't make them have to think or imagine it. They not only got to see what it looked like, but saw that I was proactive by thinking creatively and taking action. I delivered results in advance. I also looked through their eyes. How could I solve their problem, which was how to keep their audiences entertained? Taking that outlook gives a whole different perspective to the conversation. I was not asking them to hire a juggler, but to let me help them solve their problems.

Taking It Home
One thing I can guarantee you is that there are people in the world that can help you no matter what the endeavor. Your job is to make it easy for people to help you—not make them think or imagine how they can help. Help them help you. Not by telling but by showing them you are an action-taker. From the very first contact, show them the kind of person you are—the kind of person they have the option of getting involved with. It takes very little action to set yourself apart from the pack.

CHAPTER 2

Early Impactful Experiences

I have had a special combination of hard work and luck to get where I am instead of other jugglers in my home country of Holland. That's the reason why I am now the only Dutch juggler that is doing his own show internationally and was granted an "extraordinary ability work visa" from the US government. By working hard and grabbing the opportunities that have come my way, I have utilized luck to my advantage.

The nearby Rotterdam Street Theater Festival exposed me to some of the best international street performers in the world, every year. My earliest memory of seeing a live performer was at the festival when I was six years old. I watched a performer with a huge crowd. That immediately put the idea in my brain that audience participation was essential and created an extra dimension to the live shows I was seeing.

My second related memory was when I was six or seven years old and I saw a juggler at Circus Festival Monte Carlo on TV. After seeing that show, I went to my room, took what balls I could find, and tried to juggle. I got stuck since I didn't know the technique and it took me a few years before I practiced more seriously.

I first had the thought of becoming a successful international performer when I was 12 years old. Well before finishing college, this dream became a reality. And it does sometimes feel like a dream. I'd like to share with you this dream-come-true in the hopes that other young people might be inspired to follow their dreams.

My first attempt to juggle at the age of 8 *In Las Vegas, 2006*

I have achieved much in a short amount of time. Here are just a few highlights:
- Gold Medal in the 2009 Taiwan Circus Festival
- Bachelor's degree in Mechanical Engineering from the Delft University of Technology in the Netherlands, 2009 (yes, an education is important, too!)
- Guest teacher at professional circus schools, Codarts Circus School in Rotterdam, and the Fontys Circus School in Tilburg
- 3-time Guinness World Records record holder
- European representative for the International Jugglers' Association
- Two-time winner of the prestigious Merlin Award from the International Magicians Society
- Performed at the Las Vegas strip and on board the cruise ship Queen Mary 2

In Malcolm Gladwell's book *Outliers*, he discusses the idea that even more than looking at what successful people are like, look at where they are from. By that he means, "their culture, their family, their generation, and the idiosyncratic experiences of their upbringing."

Being presented with the prestigious Merlin Award for Variety Act of the Year 2012

I'd like to share with you a little more information about where I am from and what my upbringing was like.

Where I Grew Up

The Beatles had Hamburg. Bill Gates had the computer at his school. I had the metro station close to my home...

Growing up, I lived very close to a metro station. This was almost as important in shaping who I became as the yearly Rotterdam Street Theater Festival. Finding a consistent, usable space to practice is often difficult for many jugglers I know. The train station gave me almost unlimited access to an indoor place to practice. It wasn't in a bad area of town so I could practice fairly undisturbed.

Just by chance, two brothers lived five minutes by bicycle from my place and they could juggle. One was really good and could juggle 7 balls, 5 clubs, 2 diabolos, etc. When it rained, they used that metro station as their rehearsal space. They were kind to me. I must have been about 13 years old. When they went to high school and University, they stopped practicing intensively. But I continued on.

The metro station where I learned most of my tricks

When I am in town, I still use a metro station as my practice space. The first metro station I used for practice (13-18 years old) is really close to me but when I was 18 years old the police kicked me out over and over. The same officer was always on duty at that spot and he said that I should take the metro about four stops away (entering another police district) so I could try my luck there. I did so and that metro station is still my training spot when I am not performing in a theater or practicing at the government circus school.

Besides the Rotterdam Street Theater Festival, Rotterdam is also known as the "Circus Capital" of the Netherlands. I grew up and live very close to Rotterdam. In 2001, there was the European Juggling Festival. Rotterdam also has the 2nd largest youth circus in the country. When I was 13, I badly wanted to join this group. They were already full but since I kept asking my mother to call the owner over and over, he let me in. Persistence pays off.

The best juggling store in the Netherlands is also in Rotterdam. The only theater restaurant in the country that used to book variety acts on a weekly basis is located in Rotterdam. I was fortunate to work there one or two times per week for 2.5 years. This gave me a lot of stage time. Also, the setting was always the same so if a trick got a good reaction one night but not the next week, most likely it was because of my presentation. The stage, lighting, and hunger of the audience were all consistent factors.

Family vacation in the summer of 1999

My Parents

My parents were very influential. I did get a lot of parent support but I did not always see it that way. There were times that my parents provided the resistance I needed to push through. When I was younger, I often didn't see the resistance as support. But later, during critical moments, they gave certain financial gifts or lent me the money to make something happen.

My parents bought me my first set of juggling clubs that I would not have been able to afford myself. When I needed my first and second video camera to make promotional videos, they also lent me the money for it. Both times, the money for the video camera took me almost a year to pay back, but I made that work.

After I had been juggling for a few years, I told my father that Renegade clubs were the best around. This company carried a certain type of "numbers" clubs that the famous juggler, Anthony Gatto, used as well. My father had worked enough years at his job and received an extra month of pay as a bonus. He divided that between my sister, my parents, and me. I was allowed to spend it and could buy the Renegade clubs and torches if I wanted. I decided to use it differently and stick to Henry's clubs. But it was very cool of him.

My father take care of my props at the European Juggling Convention 2001

My father was a math teacher at the Rotterdam University. He spent a lot of his time in the evening preparing his lessons. I remember one time he showed me his classroom. I thought it was quite impressive. I also thought it seemed scary to have to stand for a long time in front of a group and keep them interested. I remember not being able to relate to spending years and years working in the same area in the same classroom. At least working at a primary school, the teacher moved classrooms every year. The world seemed huge and being in the classroom for years sounded like missing out on a lot of action.

My grandfather was a business owner. He ran the 2nd largest grocery shop in Den Helder. My father and uncle sometimes sold groceries in the market as teenagers. My father had said that he still was doing that in a way... but instead of groceries he now had to deliver knowledge to his clients/students. Above all, the interest of the students was more important to him than the rules management made.

My father told me a story about when he was in school and sang in its choir. One day the teacher noticed that someone was singing out of tune. It turned out to be him and he was asked to leave. He liked singing very much and it hurt him. He liked acting and singing but never pursued it thereafter. I think he got a kick out of me doing my shows instead.

My father was well-skilled in Judo, earning a 2nd degree black belt. His dream was to study for a few months in Japan. But when he was younger and had saved up enough money, he received an offer to become a teacher at a high school and he had to take that opportunity. He never made it to Japan. My first international contract with my show was performing for three months in Japan. I was proud to go there but also felt weird going there without my father. He was already sick by that time so I realized that he never would visit Japan.

I felt a bit ashamed that I could go there while it was not even my big aspiration. I wanted to have Japan on my resume. If there would have been another venue where I could get that much stage time and it looked as good on my resume, I would have been happy with that as well. Also it made me realize that if something is important to you and you get the chance you should do it. Your head and friends may tell you something else but if your heart has made the decision for you already, your only choice is to go for it. You may fail but it least you won't have to live with the regret.

Childhood

I always got picked second to last in Physical Education class. No matter how hard I tried, I just couldn't run very fast. I'd say I was below average. But then I discovered that during games with balls, I managed to throw with precision. When the other boys realized that, I moved up in the picking order.

One time during gymnastics, I got into a fight with one of my buddies. We were 10 years old. We got really angry at each other and started to fight. The teacher made us leave the gym and return to the normal classroom. As punishment, children had to write out the list with new words that we had to learn that week. So we had to write it 10 times. When we left the gym, my buddy and I weren't angry anymore and it was a bit of a bummer that we couldn't finish the game. It was close to an hour before the rest of the class would return. I said that we should start working on our punishment since otherwise we would be waiting in the classroom and doing nothing. That way we could finish it early and go home at the same time as the other kids. We did that and the teacher laughed at us and we were good to go. This is one of the first times that I remember displaying the trait of persistence and it has served me well.

With the innocence of childhood comes the belief that anything seems possible. Somehow, a lot of my friends lost that belief. I noticed that for the first time during my 3rd year at University. In secondary school, when teachers or friends of my parents said that I couldn't be a professional juggler, I didn't listen. One time, I told a teacher in the class that she should come back in 10 years time to watch my show. It felt disrespectful to speak up to an adult like that. But also I felt bad lying when my internal voice was so strong. My dream was stronger than possibly being impolite and humiliating the teacher in front of the entire class. Some people in my class laughed at me, but 10 years later that teacher has come to watch my show and is now a fan.

Street performing has been one of the best experiences of my life. It made me realize from an early age that I didn't need a company or a boss. One time when I was around 15 or 16 years old, I decided to go to town and start selling balloon animals to the kids. I made 140 USD in 2.5 hours. I sold the balloons for one dollar. Some parents got angry when I told them that the balloons weren't free. That's what they were used to

Street Performing with my buddy Chris Barning

in shopping malls. I answered that if they liked that idea of free balloons, they should write a letter to the mall and ask them to hire me. But I let them know that no one was paying me to be there. I had heard those lines from the professional buskers at the Rotterdam Street Festival and gave them a try. Also, I bought the balloons with my own pocket money and those balloons were mine. I didn't feel any obligation to have to give them away.

At the youth circus in Rotterdam, the kids that belonged to the in-crowd didn't think balloon sculpting was cool. In their eyes it was a lesser skill than acrobatics or unicycling. I remember that the teacher didn't know how to make even a simple balloon dog. But my buddy Chris Barning, who I met at the youth circus, liked it.

I was about 15 years old when Chris and I decided that we wanted to juggle full-time. The decision came to me on my way back from a gig we did together. We started a juggling duo together called Big Troubles. We did the calculations and figured out that with one gig a week we already would be able to eat, pay for the cheapest apartment to rent, and end up with a small amount for clothes. We could juggle all day and improve the act and if we got more than one gig a week, we would have money left.

Chris and I were the only two of the entire youth circus that took our skills outside of the circus club and made money with our Big Troubles juggling show. A percentage of the earliest members parents' were ex-hippies or Nouveau riche. The fact that we dared to mention that we went performing on the street and made money there was not something to be proud of. We felt awesome about running a small business and being able to attend juggling conventions and buy props by doing our shows. It was the audience supporting us and making it possible instead of only our parents.

University

I was 18 years old when I finished high school. I wanted to go and juggle professionally, but I felt insecure about it. I felt that it would take about two more years to make my act really good and become independent enough to make it all work. My mother didn't really like the idea of professional juggling and she thought it would be a great hobby and

Performing with Circus Rotjeknor in 1999

a nice side job—but not full-time. The thought of me becoming a mechanical engineer was more appealing to her. She said that if I wanted to juggle full-time, I had to move out of the house immediately and I would no longer get support from them.

I knew that I needed two more years to make the juggling work for me. Part of me wanted to go to University as well. My idea had always been to perform shows first (casinos, variety shows, cruise ships, etc.) and later in my career use juggling as a tool in my work as a speaker at corporate conventions. I figured out that University would be a good place to catch my brain up to the same level of my future audiences. If I stayed at home and went to school, I would also have additional time to work on my act and still have room and board.

Some people told me right before I graduated from high school that I would be a good teacher and should pursue that profession. I didn't want to be a high school teacher or a college math teacher like my father. I thought and still think that, for me, being a speaker is better. In a way, I still teach but I can reach more people and incorporate comedy and juggling into my speeches.

My mother always got angry when I called University my hobby and juggling my job. If I had practiced a lot and had an important exam coming up and said that I had to think of my future, she didn't really like that statement. The last couple of exams were really tough for me. They were spread apart time-wise and I had my head and schedule already more on juggling professionally than engineering. But I made it work. At the end of my time at University, I came close a few times to quitting just before the last exam. But I made it through and graduated.

Travel

I have been all over the world but my favorite countries are the Netherlands, the United States, Japan, and Australia.

I have noticed that people are quite similar all over the world. Most people want to feel safe, feel respected, and do something good for other people. Most conflicts come from the fact that people don't understand each other's motives. If you take it to the extreme: a terrorist doesn't agree with the government. He/she wants to do well for their own tribe. Most governments want to protect their citizens from terror. So there is conflict.

Cultures differ but human nature is quite similar all over the world. When basic needs like food, shelter, etc. are met people are generally friendly. But the ways they express differ and those different behaviors shape the culture. I talk about this briefly in an interview on Chinese TV which can be accessed at: www.youtube.com/watch?v=zCPbFx3GaEw.

When I performed at the theme park "Huis Ten Bosch" in Japan, there were tourists from Japan, China, Korea, and a few from Thailand. It was

In Australia with Royal Caribbean Cruises, January 2011

40 Early Impactful Experiences

Performing in Doha in 2008

really awesome. I performed a roving show throughout the park. After I finished my trick, a Thai boy, who was about 8 years old and wearing traditional clothes, bowed to me. If he would have been European, he may have clapped or given a high-five. In that moment, I realized that they had the same admiration, just a different expression.

Racism is stupid in my opinion. It's formed by the insecurity of the people that express themselves as racists. The racist leaders understand human nature so well that they use racism to inject fear into a group to be able to control that group.

When I performed in Doha, Qatar, a lot of the women were wearing burkas, which are head coverings and outer garments worn in some Islamic traditions. When I did my shows there, I couldn't see the faces of more than half of my audience members. Normally I look at facial expressions to see how I have to adjust my show to create the biggest impact for that crowd. It took me about 2-3 days to notice that I still could read the audience. The ladies that seemed interested in the show had their bodies slightly bent to the front so they could see the show better. I didn't need their facial expressions. I could judge by body position. I had never noticed that before since I had been looking at only facial expressions.

With Anthony Gatto at the Friedrichsbau Variete in Germany, 2006

CHAPTER 3

Successful Influences

With any successful endeavor, mentors are essential. I have had many, some that came across my path, and others that I sought out on my own. Whenever I had the chance, I tried to meet my mentors in real life and learn from them. I was lucky that many of my influences visited my country or lived close. Sometimes I had to fly to the other side of the world to be pushed out of my comfort zone and learn.

The "Best" –Anthony Gatto and Jason Garfield

I was a member of the Kid's Circus in Rotterdam and had persuaded the founder to expand the library of the circus club. I was their librarian at the time and had been given a budget of 200 gulden (about 100 USD). I advised the founder to get the videos, *To Be the Best* by Anthony Gatto, and *Juggling Master 2000* by Jason Garfield. I received approval. I was 14 years old at the time.

Anthony Gatto is the best juggler in the world and Jason Garfield was explaining how to juggle 1 through 11 balls in his video. Most of the budget went to shipping to get these VHS tapes sent to Rotterdam. I even had to buy a new VHS player that could play NTSC tapes, which was quite expensive. But being able to watch the two "best" jugglers in the world every day? What more did I need?

After the European Juggling Convention, the organization had agreed to write a proposal for a juggling workshop in the Netherlands with an international juggling star. I was working with them to find talent from the states, and I thought about shooting an email to Anthony Gatto to enquire of his availability. In my eyes he was a real star so he—most likely—wouldn't even answer my email. Plus, there was no way we could pay his fee. To me, Anthony Gatto was as big as Michael Jordan. So I never asked.

I had the privilege in 2006 to meet Anthony Gatto when I flew to Germany to see his act. I bought an airplane ticket to Stuttgart in Germany to see Anthony's 12-minute act. All my friends thought I was crazy to take an airplane to see a juggler work for that short of a time. It turned out that Anthony Gatto is one of the nicest people I have ever met. Most likely he wouldn't have been available to perform for the master class, but he would have answered my email.

Christopher Rodogell
— Juggler and Choreographer

There is a Mexican circus juggler about my age named Christopher Rodogell. His father owned a circus in the Netherlands. I met him on a

With my coach Christopher Rodogell in 2007

Presenting the Historical Achievement Award to Freddy Kenton in 2012 in Winston-Salem, USA

down-point in his life. He was overweight, didn't have any shows lined up, and many colleagues in the circus world didn't see his potential. By that time he also had a very bad relationship with his father. His father never officially acknowledged him as his child and hadn't paid his salary for half a season. Now Christopher is doing really well but back then, times were hard for him.

Freddy Kenton (a recipient of the International Jugglers Association's Lifetime Achievement Award) is a good friend of Christopher's father. Freddy has performed in the Moulin Rouge in Paris and many prestigious nightclubs in the world. In 2007, Freddy Kenton had expressed to Christopher that he doubted the potential of my ever becoming a showman. My juggling skills were fine already by that time, but my showmanship was still very undeveloped. Now, Freddy Kenton is my friend, coach and a great admirer. But back then, he did not see my potential.

Christopher was proud to be an "excellent choreographer" but nobody believed in his skills in that area. Christopher decided to track me down and create an act in 10 days that would prove everybody wrong. I was just preparing for a 3-month contract with Huis Ten Bosch, in Japan. Most of the routines that we intensively put together are still the routines that I work with today. Those routines have taken me to over 40 countries so far.

Steve Jobs on Strategy

Last year, I read Steve Jobs' biography. Now that I am having a bit more success with my juggling show, I suddenly have quite a few fellow entertainers contacting me on a weekly basis. Before, some of those people pointed out what I was doing wrong in their opinion (often behind my back). Others I knew only from when they contacted me on my Facebook profile.

Steve Jobs had a favorite word: bozo. The above-mentioned people were not my real friends but I used to spend too much time helping them. For example, I would take the time to recommend a certain book to read in which they could find their answers, etc. That took a lot of energy away from my own work. Those people were often unfriendly to me and sometimes their emails showed clearly that the help I gave made no impact. So I take inspiration from Steve Jobs and have learned to focus on my own goals. I am always open to helping a friend with questions and favors but am now much more careful how I choose to spend my time.

Something else I learned from Jobs was to get the best possible people on my "team." When I outsource jobs or help with my work, I am careful to pick quality people who are worth the extra money they may charge.

Valentino Bihorac – Future Inspiration

In 2001 at the EJC (European Juggling Convention) in Rotterdam, I met Valentino Bihorac (www.valentinobihorac.com). He was one of the top jugglers in Europe (performing 7 clubs, 7 clubs plus bouncing a ball on his head, and 10 rings). Valentino is four years older than me and a political refugee from Bosnia. He came to the EJC and I showed him the supermarket and places to visit around town, etc. Then Valentino invited

With Valentino Bihorac at the Palazzo Dinner Show in Vienna, Austria 2006

me to hang out with him for a week at a variety theater in Germany where he performed. That experience gave me the feel of nicer stages.

Many Mentors in Many Places

World Juggling Federation (WJF) Convention

When Jason Garfield organized the World Juggling Federation Convention in Las Vegas in 2004, he invited me to compete. While there I met such influential jugglers as Dan Holzman, Ivan Pecel, Team Rootberry, Passing Zone, and Scotty Cavanaugh.

Rootberry was teaching a master class on the Business of Juggling. That got me started on marketing and collecting good photos of my juggling throughout the years. The local juggling shop in Rotterdam (Luchtwerk) sponsored me to take this master class. Ivan Pecel, Scotty Cavanaugh and Rootberry introduced me to the concept of performing on cruise ships. Passing Zone talked about cruise ships being a good training ground to become a speaker or headliner later on. Many seeds were planted at that time.

World Juggling Federation Convention 2004 at the Riviera Hotel Casino in Las Vegas

Ivan Pecel and I winning Gold at the International Jugglers Association's Extreme Juggling Championships

Scottish Juggling Festival

February 2006, I decided to attend the Scottish Juggling Festival since Ivan Pecel was there as well and I felt it would be good to reconnect. Ivan persuaded me to attend the IJA Festival that year. I did. I hung out with Ivan in Las Vegas (his home back then) for 1.5 weeks. I won a gold medal in XJuggling at the IJA Festival. Also I got to reconnect with Dan Holzman and visit Scotty Cavanaugh in San Diego.

Important Mentors

Dan Holzman started helping me in 2010. He is the only person in the world that I have found that could and was willing to help me better the comedy in my show. He is willing to work with a non-native speaker and has the patience for it.

Because of Scotty Cavanaugh, I connected with the theme park gig at Huis Ten Bosch and got 3 months of daily stage time to build the basics of performing on a stage.

The very first cruise contract I did, I ran in into John Taylor (www.johntaylormagic.com) and Sebastian Scheepers (most experienced sound tech I know, hobby juggler, and semi-professional photographer). They helped me to better my cruise ship show and made it possible for me to have professional promotional photos using the ship's theater and lights.

Because of Team Rootberry's endorsement of the video that I shot at Theme Park Huis Ten Bosch in Japan, I was able to secure contracts with one of the three best cruise ship agents in the world.

Barry Friedman is the creator of *Get More Corporate Gigs*, which he started in 2009, right after I did my first cruise ship contract. I had my show in place. I had a venue to try out my material and shoot good video footage. It was a perfect time to put all his tips in action. Barry Friedman, along with his partner Dan Holzman, are The Raspyni Brothers, one of the most successful juggling shows around. (See www.Raspyni.com)

In 2006, certain life events started coming together for me and it pushed my show to the next level. I would like to thank Patrick Moonen for that. Patrick is one of the best hairdressers in the Netherlands, well experienced with fashion shows and TV work and he is also a good illusionist. I met him after a show I did at Casablanca Variete in

50 Successful Influences

With the Raspyni Brothers (Barry Friedman and Daniel Holzman) after my performance at the California Magic Dinner Theatre, USA

With my friend Marco Bonisimo after winning Gold at the Dutch Juggling Championships 2005

Amsterdam. Patrick helped me get my first professional promotional photos in a studio. His friend Piek who works in the studio of Erwin Olaf took those for me. I also got my first professional costume done through his network by Tycho Boeker (Prince Charming www.princecharming.nl. He normally only works with celebrities).

In that same year, I produced my first juggling DVD. Anthony Gatto and Jason Garfield had their own videos, so I wanted to have one, too. I had 500 DVDs pressed like all the professional DVDs and the Hollywood movies. Ivan Pecel, Marco Bonisimo, and Scotty Cavanaugh helped me film it.

Around the same time I met Veronique Ross when I performed at another party that year. An amateur magician who had hired me to perform for his guests held the party. Veronique Ross is the widow of two-time World Champion Magician Richard Ross and runs the Magic Art Center. The Magic Art Center is in Bennebroek and it is comparable to the Magic Castle in Hollywood. She invited me to perform at this theater. Since then I have been hanging out with magicians a lot. The fresh angle and inspiration from magicians have had a big influence. Magicians have their own shows, produce merchandise, etc. Very few jugglers I know manage to operate at that level. It inspires me to think bigger. Also the different structure and approach of setting up routines helps me to set myself apart. At the Magic Art Center I met another famous World Champion Magician, Ger Copper. Along with his partner choreographer, Roland Martis, he is helping me with new routines for my show.

I would like to thank Henk Pijper for all the support throughout the years.

Freddy Kenton is one of the most experienced jugglers I know. In 2012, I had the honor to present him with the Historical Achievement Award from the International Jugglers Association. Freddy was born in a circus setting and his parents were famous acrobats. They performed in the top shows during the high-days of variety shows. During his 60+ year career he has seen most of the best jugglers of the last century live. Freddy performed with his juggling act in the famous Moulin Rouge, Blackpool Tower, and many other prestigious venues. Freddy pushed me to start building most of my own props (using my Mechanical Engineering

With Owen Morse and Jon Wee (The Passing Zone)

Performing at the Magic Art Center in Bennebroek, 2007

Successful Influences 53

With Véronique Ross, Tony Hassini and Ger Copper

degree) thus being able to perform unique tricks. This serves me well in getting gigs in venues where they work with good jugglers on a regular basis.

I have been lucky that up until 2006 the economy was doing well and there were tons of local annual street theater festivals in Holland (sponsored by corporations and government) where I could do my solo show of 30 minutes every week (at different festivals) about 3-4 times per weekend.

The only theater restaurant in Holland that used some acts was located in Rotterdam. A waitress that worked there saw me rehearsing at the metro station very often. She had a crush on me and introduced me to the owner and I was hired. That gave me the option to do another 1-2 nights of regular shows every week (4 hours per week, a combination of close up and short stage spots).

Kaskade Magazine

I read about helpful videotape recommendations in *Kaskade*, the European juggling magazine. This magazine slowly taught me about the juggling scene. This included different conventions and festivals, as well as the direction many jugglers were taking their work. The magazine also critiques new books and videos. I bought Jason Garfield's *Juggling Master 2000* VHS after reading about it in the magazine. I read about the International Juggling Association (IJA) in the magazine.

It is important to read professionally related magazines no matter what your field of interest. The subscription fee offers a great ROI (return on investment). Every professional convention or magazine I have invested money in has helped my business.

Influences are everywhere. You can learn something from everyone you meet. Each person shapes you a bit and becomes part of your life.

CHAPTER 4

Life Strategies or How to Take Control of Your Life

Take out your notebook. There are questions here that you are going to want to answer. It's a lot easier to make changes if you have a place to record and revisit your progress.

Find a Passion or Purpose

When you grow up, sooner or later you will notice that certain things intrigue you. When you are a child and not very aware of the concepts of power and the possibilities of money, you are still very pure. The things that intrigue you during that time are not yet troubled by external influences such as peer pressure.

For me, it was a natural process toward finding what I loved to do. I just liked playing table tennis, juggling, in-line skating, and judo. What I liked about playing table tennis was the precision necessary to hit the ball a certain way and the repetitive training necessary to gain that control. That precision also came back in in-line skating. To turn the perfect 360 at the half-pipe you need practice. The challenge of trying to achieve the move was something I really enjoyed.

I found judo to be less satisfying because of the variables. In table tennis, the table is a constant factor. In in-line skating, the half pipe doesn't change. But in judo the partner you're fighting can be a bad sparring partner and if he doesn't play fair you cannot improve. You lose energy and time by this external factor.

56 Life Strategies or How to Take Control of Your Life

Posing with my juggling props, summer 1998

Juggling was the most challenging of all. It had rhythm, precision, and it had the possibility to make my skills expand to include others. In judo, for example, when one person won, the other lost. Performing juggling, the audience was most happy when the juggler succeeded.

Taking It Home
Make two columns on a page. On one side, create a list that includes activities you enjoy doing, what you are curious to learn more about, and what you do now in your free time. Opposite each item, list the skills each item involves and the qualities a person needs to pursue those further. Keep this list in plain sight so that you see it every day.

Notes:

Peer Pressure

> "Socially accepted kids are often accepted for the sheer fact that they conform well to the norms of teen culture, good and bad aspects included. Popular adolescents are more strongly associated with their peer groups' likes such as alcohol, tobacco and drugs. Some studies also show that many popular students also make lower grades than less socially accepted kids. This is possibly due to the fact that popular students may spend more time worrying about their social life rather than studying."
> —*From Wikipedia*

I have always been quite ignorant in a certain way. When students at school (13-18 years old) thought my juggling wasn't cool, I didn't care. Now, I can see why.

A beginning juggler isn't a joy to watch. At the time, I stayed focused on people like Anthony Gatto and knew I needed to work hard. The goals I was attempting weren't easy and, of course, it took time. After the juggler gets real control of his/her props it becomes spectacular to watch that juggler work. In the beginning, those students' opinions may have been accurate. What they couldn't see was the potential of becoming great and they hadn't taken that into account.

Taking It Home
If you are looking for approval from peers, always first consider the source. Is that person someone you look up to? Someone you want to be like? Make sure you can answer "yes" before you let them affect you in any way.

Notes:

With Joe Labero at his birthday party in Stockholm, Sweden

Social Media

- Use it to build relationships with people that inspire you.
- Remember that everything you post stays online forever.
- Don't say anything you wouldn't say to somebody's face.

Taking It Home

How much time a day do you spend on social media like Facebook, Twitter, texting, or email? Keep track for a week. How much of that time was entertainment and gossip? How much furthered your position in life and want you want to pursue? If they are imbalanced, make a schedule and stick to it. It's amazing how 30 minutes a day of social media, really, is plenty.

Notes:

Unhealthy Distractions

Everybody wants to be recognized for something. Not every strategy is a good choice. For example, hooking up with the wrong friends might lead you to get involved in certain behaviors. Eating yourself fat to be able to feel pity for yourself in the hope people will help you is another distraction. Getting involved in entertainment (video games, movies, etc.) as a lack or an excuse to work on your future and improve your skills or conditions isn't good either.

To me, personally, it all came down to being really scared to not go after something I really liked. If you really find what you stand for and something that you really like to do, it won't take much effort to avoid all those kinds of distractions. If you want to become good at sports, you know that eating pizza every day won't make you run faster. If you want to become good at playing an instrument, maybe popular music won't take you over completely since you will be too busy playing music yourself.

When I got more into juggling, I spent less time hanging out with those friends who were easily satisfied with playing video games. If you've found something that makes you happy and your friends start to complain that you don't spend enough time with them, then you know that those people are not your real friends. Real friends want each other to be happy and support each other.

Joe Labero

My friend, illusionist Joe Labero (www.labero.com), is a celebrity in Sweden. He is one of those entertainers who thinks on a grand scale. His shows are really big and the budgets he has to work with are large as well. He explained to me that he is extremely careful who of his colleagues he is hanging out with. It's not helpful for him to hang around colleagues that perform mostly at birthday parties.

Taking It Home:
- Jim Rohn, motivational speaker, has said that, "You are the average of the five people you spend the most time with."
- Take a good look at your closest friends. How's your average?

Voices of Negativity

Everyone I know has dealt with their own internal negative voice. Some of us are worried about what others think of us, or we create our own unpleasant thoughts. Harsh self-judgments can be abusive. And there are also many people who will say negative things to you or about you.

Taking It Home
When you are down on yourself, compliment some aspect of your personality. This can boost your self-esteem.

Learn to control your emotions. Here are some steps from Eckhart Tolle:
- Be conscious of an emotion inside you—e.g. fear or worry
- Observe it within your mind
- Notice that if you are observing it, it can't be a part of you
- Watch the emotion disappear
- As soon as you observe an emotion, you are separating yourself from it and thus it can no longer exist

Try to create a system for yourself where you know what is acceptable for you and what you would do in an ideal world. Think if you only had to prove your points to yourself. What would you do? Create this list. Read it over again. Are you really creating your list or is your list a reflection of what other people like to see?

Write down what is important to you and not what is important to your friends/bullies/etc. Thereafter, judge all the negativity by your own standards. In the end you will create the world you had written down.

Notes:

Boredom – Get Off the Couch

Find the things in life that you really like. Let's say you had all the money and time in the world: what would you spend your energy on? Once you know what that is, just doing that would be a pleasure, right? Wouldn't making this scenario a reality motivate you? Even if you're not there yet, you can take steps now to make this a reality in your life.

Taking It Home
Get off the couch. Now.

Notes:

Overcoming Fear

> Fear is an emotional state: "an unpleasant emotion caused by the belief that something is dangerous, likely to cause pain, or a threat." —*Oxford Dictionaries*

My first step in overcoming fear was deciding what I really wanted. It was overwhelming in the beginning and it would have been very comforting not to act on my new realizations. Thereafter I thought, "What would happen if I don't act on these ideas?" The result was that I wouldn't achieve anything and wouldn't get any of the results. That was equal to my worst-case scenario. I concluded that I had nothing to lose. Even failing was better than not acting since I would later know that at least I had tried. I wouldn't have to live with the regret of not having tried.

> "Courage is not the absence of fear but rather the judgment that something else is more important than fear."
> —*Ambrose Redmoon*

Taking It Home

Make a list of what you want to do/get.
- Write down what could go wrong.
- What would the consequences be if that happened?
- How bad is each consequence?
- What could you do to prevent these things from happening?
- How much energy would it take to recover from the consequence?
- When you recover from it, what might you have learned?

Most of the time the balance turns out to be quite positive and knowing that eliminates the fear.

Notes:

Change and How to Deal With It

Time causes change. Because of time our bodies change, the world changes. We can't do anything about that. As a result of that, we naturally have to change. I kind of look at it like this: when you have a computer and you don't update it, sooner or later it will stop working properly due to new settings, different programs etc. Just to keep your computer working properly you will need to update it regularly. The same goes for yourself.

Not changing is way more dangerous than changing. If I don't change, I won't be able to function in tomorrow's world. That is a given. And it is not a good option. I prefer to update myself rather than become outdated. Also, by constantly challenging yourself and learning new skills—therefore planning ahead—you can prepare yourself for the future. You can eliminate and work on all the things in your life that you are currently not happy with. Without change you won't have the potential to make your life better or more interesting.

Taking It Home
- Socially, you need to take the time to be able to keep connected and involved with what is going on around you.
- Personally, look closely at yourself and determine what you don't like about yourself. Write those things down. Look more closely and see if there is a possibility of change. If it's fixable, make a plan and stick to it. Then you can stop complaining about it.
- Over time, you may realize how important some of the things are you don't like about yourself, especially the things you can't change.

Notes:

Organizational Skills

You will need some degree of organizational skills no matter what you do. When you know what excites you and what you would love to have in your life, then you will need to think of a way to make it happen. "Organizational skills" may sound overwhelming, but it could be quite easy. For example, let's say you like darts. You will need to find out where you can practice, how you can practice more effectively, how to connect with darters that are more experienced than you and learn from them, and research where you can find them (darting club, online, etc.)? Your organizational skills enable you to create a world around you where you can do what you would like to do.

Taking It Home
- Evaluate your current organizational strategies. If you are more linear, then you will like systematic approaches using numbers and file systems and performing steps in order. If you are more global in your thinking, you will want to use a more conceptual approach by making a big-picture plan and perhaps diagramming out solutions or making categories so everything can be included.
- The best way to become more organized is to practice it in everything you do.

Notes:

Winning 1st prize for my first ship model

Using Resources Well

I don't like wasting time and I don't like wasting potential. When I do something, I want to do it well. My mother says that my grandfather was the same. He was a woodworker and carpenter. Later on he was a supervisor for constructional projects. After he retired he built models of ships from wood. Between the ages of 11 to 17, I did that as well. I did that at a model-building club. I finished 3 ships during that period. My mother told me a story that he had asked my father to get a certain type of rope for him for a ship he was working on. My father had bought the rope but it was a fraction of an inch too thick. My grandfather said that although it may have been only fraction of an inch, in full size that would have been 2 inches. So my father got him new rope. I see a lot of myself in this story.

Taking It Home
If something is important to you, don't cheat on it. Do it well or don't do it at all.

Seeking Information

Your brain is your most important asset. How you fill it determines everything in your life. It determines how you react emotionally to unforeseen situations, and how you show up for big challenges or projects. That ultimately influences the magnitude of the projects others will trust you with.

You will need to experiment and pay attention to determine how you prefer to learn and what is most effective for you in a given situation. If you want to play the piano, you could read every book on piano. But that strategy will not help you to actually play a melody well. Most likely you will need some theory on the piano and start practicing thereafter. Depending on your situation you may need to learn theory from a book in the library, the Internet, a teacher, or even meet a pianist backstage that you see who is doing a concert in your hometown. And then you will need to start practicing. You may look into lessons but you also must practice by yourself at home.

Taking It Home
See for yourself, which possibilities are in your reach at a certain time and go for the best option. When you have saved more money and other opportunities open up for better ways of learning, go for that.

Applying What You Learn

Whenever you learn new information, think about how you could implement that new information into your life. If you don't do this then taking in this new information is brain filler. Are you satisfied with that?

Taking It Home
Patience, persistence, and practice are 3 P's to remember when applying what you learn.

Notes:

Life Strategies or How to Take Control of Your Life

Speaking to People You Don't Know

For many people, there is a certain amount of fear present when speaking to someone they don't know. They may be worried about getting rejected or being put to shame. That possibility creates discomfort.

I am an introvert. I can behave like an extrovert for a certain amount of time. Introvert does not mean that I am shy. I used to be shy in certain situations. But if the outcome of the situation was and is important to me I don't have a problem speaking up, not even if the entire room thinks differently.

The fear of rejection is common. My strategy with that is to treat other people with respect, don't waste their time, and try to deliver my message as clearly and correctly as possible. If they then put me down and react impolitely, they aren't a nice person. In that case, I shouldn't be wasting my time with them. If that happens, it may not have been a nice encounter, but by the rules that the people I care about have taught me and live by—I have done right. I can always go back to that tribe with dignity.

Taking It Home
- I don't know ahead of time if a stranger will reject me. But the most important thing is to approach them from a level of respect. If you get treated badly in return, you have just learned that that person isn't worth your time to stick around.
- If you are a person who doesn't think very highly of yourself (maybe because you have been told over and over that you aren't worth much), believing and acting upon that strategy above may be hard. But if you can change your mindset, your world will change for the better.
- What I have learned from traveling around is that the core of humans are the same everywhere. Understanding the similarities in human thinking helps me to see that a stranger is not too scary to me. It's helpful in this case to have a basic understanding of the things that make humans, human.

Notes:

No Prima Donnas

Prima donna was originally a term for the leading soloist in an opera company but has been used in modern terms to describe someone who is vain, arrogant, conceited, or selfish. Some performers act like that. They want special treatment.

I see myself as a normal guy. For example, those working on a cruise ship are all there to make it a nice vacation for the passengers. In the theater, we all work to create a nice show. The lighting technician and the back-stage staff make the show possible as much as I do. During the last 1.5 years, I slowly started to realize that a lot of people aren't willing to push hard when things get tough. So it's a balancing act to motivate people to do their best quality work without being too arrogant or demanding.

Some people think they are better than other people because they hold a better job or a higher position job. I read somewhere that you can see the greatness of a man by observing how he treats the people that can do nothing for him. For example, when I am in negotiations with someone for a new project and we meet in a restaurant, I watch how they treat the wait staff. If that person treats me really well but is unfriendly to the waitress, that is a good indicator for me that they may treat me the same when I can no longer benefit them. I believe this is very shortsighted behavior. It's a red flag and I do not want this type of person on my team.

In a big project, everyone needs help from the others. You can't win a war by yourself. You need an army for that. In an army, everybody has his own task. Maybe the guy that plants the flag in the won-over-territory looks like a star, but he or she wouldn't be able to do that without the help of all the other soldiers.

Maybe the CEO of a successful company looks very important. If he gives credit for the company's results to all the people at the workforce that have made this possible, the company will thrive and be able to produce even better results in the future. Everyone in the company will feel more positive.

It's the same with my show. The lighting technician, stage staff, and consultant all work with me on my show. I am the person on stage performing it, but without their input, it would not have all come together. So it is important to give credit where credit is due. And I always remember to thank them.

Also, my name is the only one on the bill. I can tell that some stage staff are not as dedicated to my show as I am. If they make a mistake and forget to hand me a certain prop at a certain time, then I look stupid on stage. But they are anonymous in the wings so I am always grateful when it works out.

Dale Carnegie's book *How to Win Friends and Influence People* is a great read. Implementing the simple ideas described in this book can move mountains. It has done for me.

Another book I highly recommend is *From Good to Great: Why Some Companies Make the Leap ...and Others Don't* by Jim Collins. Using tough benchmarks, Collins and his research team identified a set of elite companies that made the leap to great results and sustained those results for at least fifteen years. The findings of the Good to Great study will surprise many readers and shed light on virtually every area of management strategy and practice. The findings include:

- Level 5 Leaders: The research team was shocked to discover the type of leadership required to achieve greatness.
- The Hedgehog Concept: (Simplicity within the Three Circles): To go from good to great requires transcending the curse of competence.
- A Culture of Discipline: When you combine a culture of discipline with an ethic of entrepreneurship, you get the magical alchemy of great results.
- Technology Accelerators: Good-to-great companies think differently about the role of technology.
- The Flywheel and the Doom Loop: Those who launch radical change programs and wrenching restructurings will almost certainly fail to make the leap.

Notes

Taking It Home
- Read Dale Carnegie's book.
- Look at any situation in your life through the eyes of the other party. Judge the words of someone else (especially when you're in a conflict) to form your perspective of the situation. Thereafter create an objective opinion for yourself and go for that as a solution. That way the encounter won't create problems for you in the future.

I would like to quote Will Smith:

> **"Never let the success rise to your head, and never let the failures go down to your heart."**

CHAPTER 5

Character Traits That Lead Toward Success

Weighing the Opinion of Others

One character trait that I possess is having a stubborn reaction towards other people's opinion of me. When I have been successful, some people were jealous and misled me. When I didn't do well, some people liked to put me down even more. I believe this serves to take the focus away from their own lack of achievements.

I didn't realize this when I was a kid. I probably thought that the other people, who were usually older, were most likely right. My interpretation was that I was moving in the right direction but hadn't mastered the skill yet to be complimented for the quality of my work. So I thought I just needed to keep working. It drove me to work harder. As I have gotten older, I have come to see those negative behaviors as having nothing to do with me. But I was able to make something positive come out of this misunderstanding by using it to drive me to do better.

Persistence

Just as in a previous example of fulfilling the childhood punishment after fighting with my friend, I have found that tenacity and perseverance have paid off. I have been told I have "stick-to-it-iveness." I don't give up or get easily discouraged. And I believe that this garners respects from others.

Character Traits That Lead Toward Success 73

I highly value respect. All the really valuable things in life aren't for sale. Maybe getting the latest iPhone sounds really important to you, especially since all your friends have one. Of course an iPhone is for sale but what you're really looking for (and trying to buy) is respect from those people. True respect isn't for sale. You know that you still don't truly have those people's respect because when later on a newer model iPhone comes out and you don't buy that... they still don't respect you.

You can earn respect by showing that you are worth someone's respect. That takes more courage but it has more substance and it shows your character.

Those really important things in life that you have to earn take more effort since you will have to change something from your inside (mentality, character...) and not something from the outside (cell phone, clothes...) which can't be bought.

That is why really rich people normally have a lot of respect for artists. That creativity, open-mindedness, and persistence necessary to create art can't be bought. Those qualities command respect.

With Terry Fator and his wife Taylor Makakoa before their show at the Mirage Hotel Casino in Las Vegas, 2013

Many people give circumstances only one try before giving up. Their attitude is, "That didn't work." To make most things work (even for someone that has all the experience, skill and talent), it will take more than one attempt. If you don't have the experience, most likely it will take a lot of attempts since you will need to get feedback in order to learn from your mistakes. Thereafter you will know what to do and where the difficulties are. You will know that you can make it happen. When people give up after one try, they are fulfilling the confirmation of their own statement, "That wasn't going to work anyway." And it is one less dream that they have to go after and can just give up.

I always think, "How important is this?" What if my entire world or path of my life would depend on it? Would I try harder or would I try again if the best option/scenario would become reality if only I could pull it off? Would you? And with every time you try something, the best in the world comes a bit closer to you. So the path of the rest of your life honestly does depend on it. Also, developing discipline with that one experience will pay off in all the other areas in your life.

Regarding persistence, I highly recommend Terry Fator's biography, *Who's the Dummy Now?* Terry Fator won *America's Got Talent* with his ventriloquism act and is one of the friendliest people I have ever met.

If I had kept walking in the shopping mall and never put my hat down to street perform for just 10 minutes… this book and all these adventures within its pages would have never happened.

Physical Character

Luckily, I am very healthy. I never used to be the fastest runner, but not the slowest either. When playing table tennis, judo, or in-line skating, if I practiced enough, I got better. I did get good at these activities but they never came easy. The potential in my body was there but I needed exercise and practice to bring it out.

I've been asked about my health regimen and how I keep up my energy. When making food choices, I always ask myself the question, "Would the caveman recognize it?"

When I was growing up, my mother normally cooked vegetables, some potatoes and some meat for dinner. When I am on the road it is harder. Junk food is everywhere for purchase. The healthier food is a bit more expensive but it's worth it. I think of this extra amount that I will need to spend as my "health tax".

Recently, I took part in a coaching program called www.30DaysSugarFree.com. It's something I can recommend to anyone as the benefits include better sleep, higher energy, and better overall health. It is also common for people to lose weight when doing this program.

I always try to sleep about 8 hours per night. I don't like to go to sleep after 1 AM but I don't mind getting up early—if necessary. I found for myself that if I work really long hours—for example until 4 AM—the next day I am so tired that I feel I lose that day entirely. When I am not under a major deadline it is better to get enough sleep so the time working the next day is more effectively spent.

Regarding exercise, I am lucky that juggling is an exercise in itself and I really enjoy doing it. I try to practice about 2.5 hours a day. Juggling is a low-intensity, interval training that involves balance, concentration and endurance. If I train with weights on top of my daily juggling practice I get too tired and my muscles get unusable for juggling for a few days. During a period in my life I juggled for 3 hours a day and went to the gym for 2 hours per day. The result was that I had to sleep for 10-11 hours a day. This may have been great for my condition and juggling skill, but I didn't get many other things done during that time. I cut back on the fitness part which was a better balance for me. My body didn't need that much time each day anymore to recover so I could spend that energy on other projects that were important to me as well. Balance is important. Put your energy on projects that are important to you.

Mental Character

I managed to graduate from the Delft University of Technology with a Bachelor Degree in Mechanical Engineering. I think that my brains work well. There are smarter people out there, but not everybody uses their brains well. I do believe that having a well functioning left side of the brain is important to oversee the big picture and help to predict the consequences of your actions. But the right side is needed to bring in the passion and preferences, while the left side works on the situation.

If you have a great idea you will need to bring it to reality. I think that is our goal/purpose as human beings. What is there about you that can make the world better? Perhaps it's saving resources or improving happiness for other people through a new product or system. That idea gets developed by the right side of your brain. But when you don't let your left side work on the logistics of how to bring this spark of genius into reality, all is worthless. When you don't act on this idea and let the opportunity go wasted, nothing has changed in the world. As Steve Jobs said, "You haven't put a dent in the universe."

My coach, Dan Holzman, thinks of your brain and the creative ideas it comes up with as a muscle. If you regularly train your muscles, you will get stronger. If you train your thinking, you will come up with more original ideas.

It is really important to know when to persist with something to make it work. Not everything is easy and most of the time, to reach greatness, it takes a lot of persistence. But if you clearly see that you're "beating a dead horse," please quit the project as soon as possible and invest your time in something else.

I have practiced my left brain thinking skills at school for about 20 years. Now I am using my right brain more to create ideas for acts, routines, jokes, and clever business ideas for the promotion of my shows. This has turned out to be a great combination for me.

Emotional Character

Education has helped me a lot in the area of emotional character. For example, after listening to Tom Hopkins audio book on selling, getting rejected isn't too big of a deal anymore emotionally. I believe I am more of an introvert, which is great. One example is that I need to spend a lot of time practicing alone on the craft of juggling. Most of the time I travel alone. This is not hard for me and an important trait in my line of work.

When confronted with big emotions like disappointment, conflict, or sadness, I often turn to practice my juggling. My practice is an outlet for these emotions. I also try to use these emotions as inspiration to answer two questions: "What's bigger? What's better?" I bring these questions into my work often. These are inspired by one of my mentors, Barry Friedman, who constantly repeats this in his Showbiz Blueprint course. Of all my mentors, he has had the biggest impact on my education after graduating from University.

And of course, I give my mother a call. It's important to have someone you can call.

On Success

The best things aren't for sale. Getting good at something is one of those things. You will need to earn it.

> **The definition of success is, "the accomplishment of an aim or purpose."** —*Oxford Dictionaries*

Is your aim or purpose an internal or external one? In other words, do you feel connected to your goal or are you just pursuing something to impress the people around you? In the first situation, it is much easier to accomplish your goal.

The words success and succeed are really close to each other. To get success you will need to succeed. If you look at those words you will realize that something won't come to you with the first attempt. To succeed you will need to show persistence. It's like a wall around a backyard. If you don't want to be inside the backyard, you will need to climb over the wall. That takes some effort. The wall is only there to filter out the people that aren't willing to take the effort to be worthy of the success.

A TED video inspired me toward this way of thinking. The title is, Randy Pausch: *Really Achieving Your Childhood Dreams*. Here is a link to the talk: http://www.ted.com/talks/randy_pausch_really_achieving_your_childhood_dreams.html

Owning something doesn't make you better. Being better makes you better.

Taking Action

Don't be scared to start. You actually may get want you want. Realizing that you may succeed can be scary.

The first place to start is with something small. In Japan, there is an expression that if somebody walks in the moisture for long enough, he or she will get wet as well.

Move into the direction of something you want. What if you want to learn to juggle? If you don't have money for juggling balls and your father doesn't allow you to buy them, practice with balls of socks, stones, oranges, or anything you can throw or manipulate.

Sometimes you have to break some rules. Make sure that you don't hurt or ruin somebody else with that permanently.

Some years ago I came up with the following idea. If I don't act on an idea I—of course—won't get the outcome and the success of that idea. If I try and I succeed, it results in the outcome that I hoped for. If I try and fail, at least I won't have to live with the regret of not having tried and I may have learned something. Following this analogy made going after new ideas a no-brainer for my personal ideas. Not taking action guaranteed the worst possible outcome, so I had nothing to lose.

Taking a small step still is better than doing nothing. I remember magician, Jeff McBride, saying in an interview that every second he has a deck of cards in his hands he is a second further in skills than the guy that didn't have cards in his hands during that time.

In Jason Garfield's tape, *Juggling Master 2000*, (that I watched every day as a teenager), he said that each day he didn't practice, it would take a day longer for him to master a certain trick. And, it might be even longer because when he missed a day, he needed to make up for the slight disimprovement that happened during that day as well.

Two months ago I read the book, *The Dip*, written by Seth Godin. It was helpful in terms of setbacks along one's path and discovering

Character Traits That Lead Toward Success 79

After my performance at Jeff McBride's night club Wonderground in Las Vegas in 2011

continued motivation. If you don't find the exact steps you need to take to get somewhere, that is okay, as long as you are headed in the direction that you want to go.

There is possibility and opportunity in everything around you. Keep your eyes open. Don't be afraid to ask questions. A mistake is a lesson to learn from. Success is confirmation you did something right.

If you have a chance, I recommend *Poke the Box*, by Seth Godin who writes about failure and its importance toward success.

Remember: Whatever you try ...by trying, you always win.

BONUS

Learn to Juggle

By now you have read an entire book about the life lessons and adventures that I have experienced through juggling. Although these or similar lessons can be learned through any activity that's practiced with full commitment, my guess is that—since you decided to read this bonus chapter—by now you want to learn how to juggle!

Juggling Instruction

At my Youtube-page (www.youtube.com/nielsduinker), I have posted a series of free tutorials that will get you started on the basics of juggling. These videos can also be watched through this special page at my website: www.nielsduinker.com/learn-to-juggle.

If after watching you're hungry to learn more you can also take a look at the *Learn To Juggle* DVD that I have available in the webshop of my website.

Benefits of Juggling

There are many benefits that can be experienced through juggling.
- An engaging activity in which you exercise your mind and body at the same time.
- Helps you practice focus and concentration.

Juggling in Singapore, 2012

- Improves balance, rhythm and coordination in the body.
- Many sports coaches recommend that their athletes take up juggling.
- Proven to increase the amount of gray matter in the brain (*Nature* magazine, volume 427, Jan. 2004).
- Research suggests it may prevent Alzheimer's disease.
- A portable workout. The equipment required for juggling is minimal and portable. This makes it a perfect exercise for business travelers or a fun activity to do during lunch break at school. It also helps you clear your mind and be able to tackle your job or homework with more clarity and focus.
- Stress Relief—When you are learning to juggle, you are immediately absorbed in the activity. It's almost impossible to think of anything but the task at hand. This makes it a great way to escape any worries, stress, or anything that might be hanging over your head!

If you are interested in learning more about the benefits of juggling, please visit these websites:

http://www.howstuffworks.com/leisure/brain-games/juggling-exercise-brain.htm

http://www.oddballjuggling.com/juggling-for-kids/

http://www.juggling.org/jw/86/1/health.html

http://www.lifehack.org/articles/lifestyle/learn-how-to-juggle-and-improve-your-brains-power.html

Suggested Resources

Books
Motivational and Self-Improvement
Carnegie, Dale. *How to Win Friends and Influence People.* New York: Simon and Schuster, 1937.

Collins, Jim. *Good to Great: Why Some Companies Make the Leap ...and Others Don't.* New York: HarperCollins Publishers, 2011.

Fator, Terry. *Who's the Dummy Now?* Australia: New Holland Australia, 2008.
- The benefits of persistence.

Ferriss, Timothy. *The 4-Hour Workweek: Escape 9-5, Live Anywhere, and Join the New Rich.* New York: Random House, 2009.
- Introduction in the art of outsourcing as well as becoming a successful entrepreneur.

Godin, Seth. *The Dip.* New York: Penguin Group (USA), 2007.
- Motivation enhancer.

Hopkins, Tom. *How to Master the Art of Selling.* New York: Hachette Book Group, 2005.

Isaacson, Walter. *Steve Jobs.* New York: Simon and Schuster, 2011.
- Helpful on many levels of business. Emphasized the need to be quick with decisions to be successful.

Kiyosaki, Robert T. *Rich Dad, Poor Dad*. Scottsdale, AZ: Plata Publishing, 2011.
- Find the best consultants you can find and pay them well.

Juggling

Clark, Shaun. *Cigar Box of Tricks*. United Kingdom: Circustuff, 1994.

Dancey, Charlie. *Encyclopedia of Ball Juggling*. California: Butterfingers, 1994.

Ernest, James. *Contact Juggling*. Ernest Graphics Press, 2011.

Sikkel, Manon, and Michiel Klonhammer. *Jongleren*. Netherlands. http://www.bol.com/nl/p/jongleren/1001004001546268/
- Introduction to the history of juggling and many beginning juggling tricks. Good foundation on the art of juggling and right attitude towards juggling.

Magazines

JUGGLE magazine
http://jugglemagazine.com/
- Learn more about the American juggling scene.

Kaskade Juggling Magazine
http://www.kaskade.de/en
- Learn more about the international juggling scene

Websites

How to Master the Art of Selling Anything, website of Tom Hopkins
http://www.tomhopkins.com/p/1032.html
- Learn more about selling and create a workable mindset towards rejection.

Get More Corporate Gigs, website of Barry Friedman
www.GetMoreCorporateGigs.com
- A self-guided course on how to book your show.

ShowBiz Blueprint, website of Barry Friedman
www.ShowBizBlueprint.com
- For serious performers who want to take their show to the next level.

30 Days Sugar Free, website of Barry Friedman
www.30DaysSugarFree.com
- Support for individuals through the transformational journey of living 30 Days Sugar Free with world-class coaching, a vibrant online community, recipes, personal support, and weekly telephone conference calls.

Magic and Illusion, about.com internet article
http://magic.about.com/od/magicreview/fr/050506festent.htm
- How to approach festivals, theme parks, etc. with cold-emailing and getting success. Not trying is guaranteed failure.

Videos

Niels Duinker YouTube Series
www.youtube.com/nielsduinker
- Anyone can learn how to juggle by watching my recent youtube series:

Niels Duinker Interview on Chinese TV
www.youtube.com/watch?v=zCPbFx3GaEw

To Be The Best, by Anthony Gatto
- A thorough guide for learning how to structure practice sessions.

In Talinn, Estonia

Niels Duinker's Resume

Casinos / Theme Parks / Dinner Shows

Holland Casino, the Netherlands
Huis Ten Bosch Theme Park, Nagasaki – Japan
Planet Hollywood, Las Vegas (guest at the Nathan Burton show)
Riviera Hotel en Casino, Las Vegas – USA
Vegas Wonderground, Las Vegas – USA
"De Heksenkethel" Theater Restaurant – the Netherlands
"Saudi Arabian Oil Company" gala dinner, Hotel Okura Amsterdam
Studio21 Event Diner Show, Hilversum – the Netherlands
California Magic Dinner Theater, San Francisco – USA
Park Bellewaerde, Belgium
Slagharen Theme Park, The Netherlands
Scheinbar Variete Theater, Berlin Germany

Cruise Ships

Crystal Cruise Line
Oceania Cruises
Holland America Cruise Line
Norwegian Cruise Line
Celebrity Cruise Line
Princess Cruise Line
Regent Cruise Line
Royal Caribbean Cruise Line
Cunard Cruise Line
Carnival Cruise Line
Disney Cruise Line

Festivals

Souk Waqif Festival, Doha Qatar
October Festival, Sasebo Japan
Moisture Festival 2013, Seattle USA
Rotterdam International Street Theater Festival, the Netherlands
Dreamhack 2011, Sweden
Dutch National Magic Championships, the Netherlands
– Special Guest
TEDxAmsterdam, the Netherlands
Alkmaar Street Theater Festival, the Netherlands
– People's Choice Award
Pilot Festival for World EXPO, Shanghai China
International EXPO2011, Xi'an China
British Juggling Festival, England – Special Guest
International Jugglers' Association Festival, United States
– Special Guest
Chinese Taipei Acrobats Association Festival, Taiwan
International Jugglers Assocation (IJA) Festival 2008
– Invited guests Cascade of Stars show

Awards

Recognition: USA work visa 2013-2016 "O-1 Visa: Individuals with Extraordinary Ability"
"Variety Act of the Year" – International Magicians Society, 2012
Guinness World Records, record holder, 2011
2-time Guinness World Records, record holder, 2012
Guinness Book of World Records, record holder, 2013
World Juggling Federation Championships 2004, United States
– Silver Medal
National Juggling Championships 2005, The Netherlands
– Gold Medal
National Juggling Championships 2005, The Netherlands
– Gold Medal (2x)
International Jugglers' Association 2006, Extreme Juggling
– Gold Medal
National Juggling Championships 2007, The Netherlands
– Gold Medal
National Juggling Championships 2009, The Netherlands
– Silver Medal
National Juggling Championships 2011, The Netherlands
– Silver Medal
Taiwan Circus Festival 2009 – Golden Award
Taiwan Circus Festival 2009 – Award for the best Juggler
Japan Juggling Championships 2009, 5 clubs – Silver Medal
Street Theater Festival Dronten 2005, The Netherlands
– Special Recognition Award
Street Theater Festival Alkmaar 2005, The Netherlands
– People's Choice Award
Street Theater Festival Kunstkop 2001, The Netherlands
– First Prize

Teaching
Codarts University of the Arts, Rotterdam – the Netherlands
Fontys University of Applied Sciences, Tilburg – the Netherlands
ROC Eindhoven College of Leisure, Sport & Security – the Netherlands
National Taiwan College of Performing Art, Taipei – Taiwan
Annual Event – International Jugglers' Associaton, Lexington – USA
Annual Event – World Juggling Federation, Las Vegas – USA

Corporate Clients include:
Coca Cola Company
Shell
Intel
Saudi Arabian Oil Company
Mitsubishi
ABN AMRO
Athlon Car Lease
Campina
CNV
DSM
Yokogawa
Getronics
Ikea
KLM Airways
Unilever
QPAD
Xerox

Performing 7 clubs for the first time on stage for 2,500 colleauges. European Juggling Convention 2003 in Denmark. August 9th, I turned 18 that day.

Performing 8 rings at the "Cascade of Stars" Show at the Lexington Opera House

Newspaper articles from Holland and the Middle East

St Petersburg, Russia

Paris, France

102 Niels Duinker's Resume

Summer 2012 with the remainder of the Northern Polar Ice in the background

Close to Antarctica with the penguins

Niels Duinker's Resume

Shanghai, China

Petra, Jordan

Copenhagen streetshow

In the Bahamas while performing on board a cruise ship, 2013

Acknowledgements

My parents
Iris Duinker
Henk Pijper
Robin Matrix
Jan Kieft (Luchtwerk)
Anthony Gatto
Barry Friedman
Daniel Holzman
Annie Keeling
Driekus Heijsteeg
Johan Both (Circus Rotjeknor)
Bouke van Tongeren
Koert van Eijk
Ger Copper
Roland Martis
Freddy Kenton
Karl-Heinz Ziethen
Joanie Spina
Codarts University for the Arts
Hans Klok
Adam Fields
Dick Franco
David Marchant
Steve Russell
Jeff Civillico
Michael Chirrick
Sebastian Scheepers
John Taylor

www.nielsduinker.com

www.ingramcontent.com/pod-product-compliance
Lightning Source LLC
LaVergne TN
LVHW051846080426
835512LV00018B/3097